Everyone's Guide to

PASTEL PAINTING

pbi publishing

Printed and bound for Philip Berrill International Ltd
P.O. Box 39, Southport PR8 4ZZ, England
bySTIGE, Italy.
Photography by Peter Raymond, Southport.
Origination by DL Repro Ltd., London EC1M 4DD.
Typeset by John O'Hanlon, Southport.
ISBN 0-9541323-3-5

The Conté range of pastels and Winsor and Newton
artists' materials are used throughout this book and
are recommended by artist Philip Berrill.

CONTENTS

EVERYONE'S GUIDE TO PASTEL PAINTING
CONTAINS 27 DEMONSTRATIONS FOR YOU
TO TRY

Philip Berrill "The Flying Artist"

Philip Berrill was born in 1945 in Northampton. Philip is a professional artist, art tutor, lecturer, and author whose techniques and methods of learning to paint are taught and enjoyed worldwide. Philip now lives in Southport with his wife Sylvia. They have a daughter Penelope. Philip first recalls discovering paint from the age of three. It was one sunny afternoon. Philip wandered into his father's glasshouse. At the end of the glasshouse stood a large bucket of whitewash and a tubular pump-type sprayer. Philip loaded it with whitewash from the bucket and had a lovely afternoon spraying all his father's best tomatoes and plants white. The entire inside of the glasshouse was covered with whitewash . Philip had discovered paint, and that with paint you could change the world. His father returned to find his glasshouse a white house and his son drippping from head to foot with whitewash, a white paint.

At the age of 14 Philip decided he wanted to make a living as a professional artist, having always enjoyed art at school where he came under the influence, and studied under, the Welsh artist and tutor, John Sullivan. Philip's love and enthusiasm for sketching and painting is infectious. He believes that art should be for everyone and enjoys passing on his enthusiasm to people of all ages. His art courses, TV art series and "Painting for Pleasure" Roadshows have always proved popular and in great demand worldwide.

Philip held his first one - man exhibition at the age of 18. Other group and one - man exhibitions followed.

Philip Berrill painting during a 12-hour painting marathon session he did for a television Telethon.

When he was 28 a major exhibition of his work was held at Liverpool University. It was opened by the renowned BBC radio and TV broadcaster Brian Redhead. As a direct result of this exhibition Philip realised his ambition to become established as a professional artist and launched his very successful art classes using his own special approach to teaching sketching and painting. These proved so popular the artist developed his worldwide correspondence art courses. In the 1980s painting holiday courses in Great Britain followed and these led to organising and tutoring on painting holiday courses in Europe, in Rome, Venice, Florence and Paris. Philip was invited to lecture and demonstrate painting on sea cruises. Demonstration and lecture visits followed to Houston, Dallas and Dubai. Philip's exhibition, 'The Italian Connection' an exhibition of his sketches and paintings of his Italian journeys and other European locations was very well received.

Philip enjoys painting everything from miniatures to murals. His paintings and signed limited edition prints are owned by patrons and galleries worldwide. His murals are found in private and public locations.

Philip, whose sketching and painting courses and techniques are designed to be suitable for people of all abilities and all ages, found great enjoyment in the challenge of producing his own art videos. These led to the invitation to produce and present his own 13 - part television series, "Paint with The Flying Artist", and now to the invitation to write and illustrate his own series of art books specially for you. The books "Everyone Guide to ..." are designed to cover a wide range of mediums, techniques and subjects to introduce you to the joy and pleasure of sketching and painting.

Top right. Teenagers enjoying one of Philip's pastel demonstrations.

Right. Philip prepares an assessment for one of his correspondence art course pupils.

Below. A pastel study by Philip Berrill

Introduction

Have you have ever stopped to watch an artist creating a picture with coloured chalks on a pavement? Perhaps you have been on holiday and have seen artists offering to sketch and paint your own, or a member of your family's, portrait in black and white or coloured pastels ? If so, the chances are that you, like myself, have become entranced by the medium of pastels.

I am delighted to say that pastels are once again becoming a popular medium for artists, students and leisure painters. Most people are familiar with water colours, oil painting and sketching. Sometimes a medium can drift out of fashion, only to be re-discovered by a future generation when it gains a new and fresh popularity.

Part of the joy of working with pastels is their versatility and potential for picture making. Pastels offer scope for the individual's freedom of expression and style. They lend themselves to the rendering of almost all subjects. I hope that through reading "Everyone's Guide to Pastel Painting" they will weave their charm on you, and that you will spend many enjoyable hours exploring this captivating medium.

Pastels are robust and durable, especially if due care is given to storing or framing the finished work. Pastels are remarkably easy to learn to use. The demonstrations in this book are designed for you to try out in the order they appear. In this way they will introduce you to the various types of pastels, providing you with a range of techniques that will enable you to produce your own original studies.

Pastels can be gloriously messy, but by taking the appropriate steps pastel pictures can be produced with remarkably little fuss or mess.

The term pastel painting is used mainly for the technique in which the artist gently rubs and blends the pastel either with a fingertip, or with a pointed, long or short, firm, blending stick made from soft paper or chamois leather called a stub or a tortillon. We shall look at at this technique, but we will also explore pastel sketching and other techniques in which the pastel is not rubbed. This book is designed to introduce you to the widest possible range of pastel techniques, enabling you to catch the essence of a subject with just a few strokes of a pastel, to produce a preliminary sketch as the basis for a main picture, or to produce finished pastel pictures.

Pastels are an ideal medium to use at home, in a classroom or art studio. They are also an excellent medium for taking out-of-doors on sketching and painting expeditions. The materials occupy little space, and so are convenient to carry with you, or to store away.

I often find teenagers, whose concepts of art are not yet firmly fixed and are keen to explore all art media forms, have an immediate feel for pastels. Most adults think in terms of the traditional mediums of water colours, oil paints and acrylics for picture making. I often notice that when adults come on one of my pastel courses for the first time, they are surprised that they have overlooked pastels and enjoy the versatility of the medium.

If you are a beginner, this is a splendid medium to start with. If you are a painter but have not tried pastels, I feel confident you will enjoy the experience when you try them. If you already use pastels, this book will introduce you to some new ideas and approaches to the medium and will help you develop your skills still further.

The enticing look of pastels

Students, Jane, Sheila and Nathaniel, members of one of Philip Berrill's art classes, watch as Philip gives some finishing touch advice.

Pastel Materials and Equipment

PASTEL MATERIALS AND EQUIPMENT

One of the great joys of pastels is that not only is it an inexpensive medium , but you can start with the minimum of materials. A sheet of grey pastel paper and a black and a white Conté pastel are all you need to start. There is considerable wisdom in starting with just the basic materials and gradually adding to them; this way you build your own collection of pastels and materials to suit your own personal preference. The following description of pastel materials will give you a full understanding of what is available. I will also list the items I suggest you gather to make the Essential Pastel Kit with which to start.

SOFT PASTELS

Soft pastels are made from a mixture of very fine pigment, chalk and pipe clay mixed with water. They do not deteriorate with age and the finished painting will not crack, fade or darken over the years. A pastel picture can retain the look and freshness of the day it was finished. Soft pastels usually come in round stick form. They are soft, powdery and are applied directly to the paper. Delightful effects can be achieved by gently rubbing one pastel colour on top of another. Conté pastels can be obtained individually or in sets of 12, 24 or 48.

FIRM PASTELS

Firm or hard pastels usually come in square stick form and are essentially chalk based. The most popular are the Conté Carres pastels or crayons. They are ideal for pastel drawing , pastel sketching and detailed work, as confident, firm line or detail can be produced when required.   These firmer pastels are less smudgy than soft round pastels, and whilst they can be blended by laying one colour on top of another,   they do not lend themselves so readily to blending with the finger. Picasso, Degas, Delacroix and many other great masters of the past century have used the Conté Carres, which can be obtained individually or in sets of 12, 24 or 48.

Different opportunities are offered to the artist by the firmness or softness of the pastel chosen.

PASTEL PENCILS

Pastel pencils are firm or hard pastels encased in wood, in the same manner as the traditional graphite pencil. Pastel pencils are useful for the

artist wanting to make more detailed studies but where the velvety pastel look is required. The point of the pastel pencil can help give the detail more easily. Animal and bird studies, in which the effects of fur and feather are important, are good examples of subjects often rendered in pastel pencil. Most artists collect together a mixture of soft, hard and pastel pencils. They can be intermixed.

OIL PASTELS

These are quite different from soft pastels, and should not be confused with them. However, as they are called pastels, I will explain more about them and give details on how to use them in the later sections of this book.

PASTEL PAPER

The soft and powdery nature of pastels means that they need a paper with a slight texture, what artists call 'tooth', to enable the pastels to grip the surface. A smooth or shiny surface is not recommended. Pastel paper is often known as Ingres paper. It comes in a wide range of colours and is produced by a wide range of art paper manufacturers. Some pastel techniques, especially the pastel sketching technique, provide the opportunity to let the background colour of the paper show through, and thus become an integral part of the whole picture. In such instances the colour of paper you choose is important. In the pastel painting technique the whole surface of the painting is usually covered, leaving no paper exposed. On these occasions the colour is less important.

It is possible to use paper known as sugar paper for trying out ideas and pastel sketches. Scrap books and newspaper cutting books available from most art shops and stationers can provide an inexpensive source of paper. However, for finished and important studies buy Ingres paper. The colour of the paper is less likely to fade in any areas you may wish to leave exposed.

Pastel paper comes in sheet, sketch pad and sketchbook form. Look carefully at the colours in the pad to ensure they are colours you feel you will be comfortable working on. A selection of pale and medium greys, pale bluish-grey, cream, ivory, a dark green and crimson are amongst the most suitable to start with. The choice of colour and texture is a personal one. Try to ensure that your pastel paper is at least 80 gsm or above in weight. This will ensure it is substantial enough for you to work on. An ideal weight is 170gsm. Winsor and Newton Art Media paper comes in an extensive range of colours in sheet and pad form.

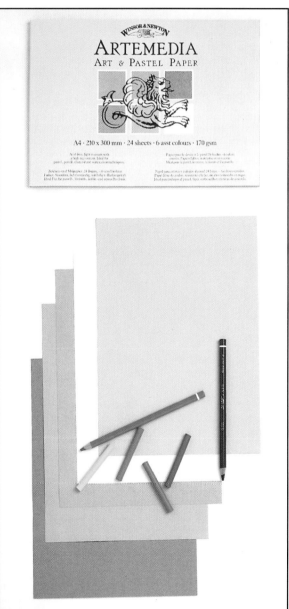

MISTAKES, ERASERS AND A BRUSH

There will be occasions when you make a mistake, or you decide that you would like to change part of a pastel picture. Do not try rubbing out with a normal eraser. The pastel will almost certainly smudge and could look unpleasant. To correct an error, or to make a change, use a clean, dry, round, hog bristle, nylon or synthetic hair paintbrush. Gently jab at the area to be changed. This will loosen and dislodge the surface pastel. Blow this away from the picture and then use a soft putty eraser to remove the remainder. The item, area or passage of work can then be reworked.

FIXATIVE

When the pastel picture is finished there is always a risk of it being smudged accidentally. A clear fixative is often used by pastel artists to hold the loose particles of pastel to the surface of the picture. Fixative normally comes in "ozone friendly" aerosol cans and is very convenient to use in this form. However it can also be obtained in bottle form. A tubular mouthpiece can be used to apply a spray of fixative. Some artists prefer not to fix their pastel studies as they believe the picture loses a little of its freshness. The choice is a personal one, but I do use the aerosol fixative.

BOXES AND THE CARE OF PASTELS

Loose pastels can become soiled and grubby as colour is transfered from the sides of one colour to another by the fingers. I suggest that you find a soft, shallow, plastic box complete with a press - on lid. The box needs to be no larger than $9\frac{1}{2}$" x 6"x 3", 240mm x 150mm x 75mm. Line the box with a piece of stiff netting, or rug making canvas so that the sides come almost to the top. Half fill the box with ground rice and place your soft pastels in the box. This will keep them remarkably clean. The sides of the stiff netting or rug can be pulled upwards to bring your pastels to the surface when you wish to work with them. When you have finished, press on the box top and place several thick rubber bands round the box so that the lid does not accidentally open. Gently shake the pastels back into the ground rice.

Loose pastels stored and kept clean in a plastic box of ground rice

DRAWING BOARD

Many people like to work flat on a table, while others prefer to stand and work at an easel. In either situation you will require a rigid surface on which to work. The surface will need to stand the firm pressure that you will often be applying when you work with pastels.

Pastel sketch pads are quite rigid, especially if working flat on a table. Use a bulldog clip or a little sticky tape to secure the loose end of the page you are working on. However, if you take a page out of the sketch pad to work on, or buy paper by the sheet, you will need a good drawing board. These need not be too expensive and can be obtained from most art shops or stationery stores. Drawing boards are made from laminated wood or white plastic covered chipboard. Do not use drawing pins; use drawing board clips or plastic masking tape to hold the paper to the surface. If you are going to take your drawing board on painting trips out-of-doors, or to an art class, you do not want a board that is too heavy. Smooth brown hardboard is the answer, as it is lightweight, inexpensive, and can be obtained from most 'Do it Yourself' stores, often as off-cuts. I would suggest a piece 18" x 14", 457mm x 356mm but if you work on a larger scale, invest in a larger piece of hardboard.

Drawing board

NEWSPAPER

For some artists a drawing board can be too firm a surface to work on. The soft, cushion-like effect when using a pastel sketch pad can be quite pleasant. If you want to create the same cushion - like effect, lay 10 or 12 sheets of newspaper on your drawing board before fixing your sheet of pastel paper on top.

Drawing board with newspaper

PORTFOLIO

Pastel pictures should be kept clean and flat, ideally in a portfolio. To ensure that one pastel picture does not transfer colour to the back of another one in the portfolio I recommend that you cut a piece of greaseproof paper to the same size as the picture. Use a paperclip at each corner to fix the protective greaseproof paper to the pastel study.

Pastel and drawing board

EASELS

If you would like to work at an easel, you need to decide if you plan to sit down or stand up. It may be that you would like the freedom to do both.

Winsor and Newton's "Tay" table easel is an excellent easel for the artist wishing to work indoors. It can be set at different angles and can be folded flat for storing. It is wide enough to support a drawing board or pastel sketch pad. The easel is also rigid enough to work on.

For indoor or outdoor work I recommend the wooden Winsor and Newton "Severn" sketching easel, or the metal "Trent" easel. These can be positioned for working standing up or lowered to sit at. They can be set in a table flat position. They are light enough to carry, yet rigid enough to work on, leaving both hands free to hold and work with the pastels. They will collapse making them compact and easily transportable.

SUNDRY ITEMS

A 2B graphite pencil, a small A5 cartridge sketch pad and a fine, black felt-tip, or nylon-tip, pen are well worth having with you for making sketches and notes of suitable subjects. A bag or satchel divided into sections to take your pastel sketchbook, pastels, fixative and other pastel materials helps keep everything neat and tidy. Suitable bags can be found in most art shops, fishing tackle shops and camping shops. Ensure that your name and telephone number are marked inside the bag so that if you misplace it, the finder can make contact with you to arrange its safe return.

Table easel

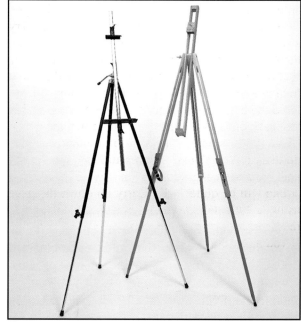
Sketching easel

THE ESSENTIAL PASTEL KIT

I suggest the following items:

A box of 12 assorted Conté soft pastels, an extra stick of white pastel, an A4 pad of Winsor and Newton Media pastel paper, a Conté tortillon or stub, a putty eraser, a Winsor and Newton round, No. 6 Cotman or Sceptre paint brush, an aerosol can of Winsor and Newton fixative.

The above makes an excellent starting kit but I recommend you add the following items:

A medium stick of charcoal, a small stick of Conté black, sanguine, sepia and white Conté Carres or miniature hard pastels, a box of 12 assorted Conté pastel pencils and a portfolio in which to keep your finished work.

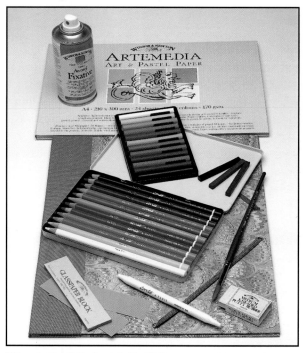
The essential sketching kit

Demonstration 1
Pastel Strokes and Pastel Marks

Play with the pastels to see how many effects you can create. Take a brown, round or square pastel, snap it into three pieces of differing length, short, medium and long. Take the medium piece between your thumb and forefinger and with the top edge of the pastel make long, medium and short downward strokes on a cream, or light-coloured, pastel paper. Try hatching, that is a series of parallel lines. Try crosshatching, where you make hatching lines and then cross other parallel lines over the original lines in a different direction. Jab the pastel at the paper to create dots, otherwise known as stippling.

Hold the pastel so that the long side of the pastel is touching the paper. Pull the pastel down the paper. Make long, medium and short side strokes. Now do that again with a lot of pressure from your hand and fingers on the pastel. The tone of the pastel stroke will be quite dark. Carry on down the page using a little less pressure, which should give a medium tone, or strength, of the pastel colour.

If you have round and square pastels, do this with a stick of each pastel.

Pastels shown broken into pieces

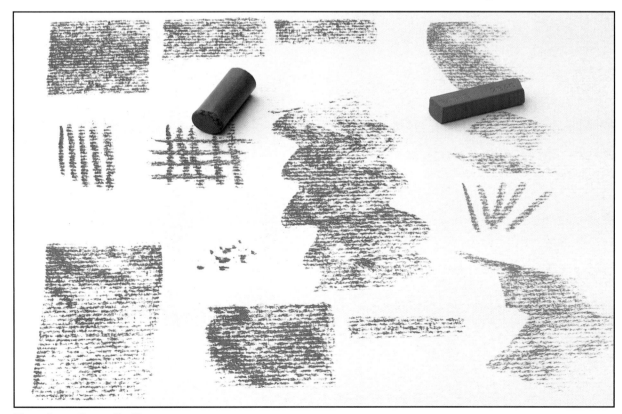

Pastel marks and effects

Demonstration 2
Shaping Pastels

Pastels come in varying degrees of softness or firmness depending on the manufacturer. Some makes are very soft, others are quite hard. Conté round and square pastels, the ones I use, are soft, but a little firmer than the very soft pastels. The Conté pastels allow artist to shape the ends offering scope for even more types of marks and effects.

Top and bottom right. I show how, with a craft knife, you can carefully shape round and square pastels to a point, or to a chisel-edge. Glass paper can be used to help shape a pastel end, or to re-sharpen the right-angled edges of the sides of a square pastel if they are worn away with use.

Experiment with the top edges, sides and shaped ends of your pastels to see if you can create effects and marks in the way I show below.

HANDY HINT. To prevent pastels from smudging they should be spray fixed. Details of how to do this can be found on page 62.

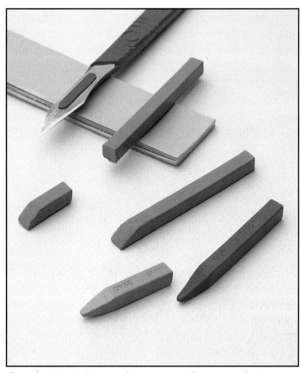
Square pastels - end you can shape

Effects and marks

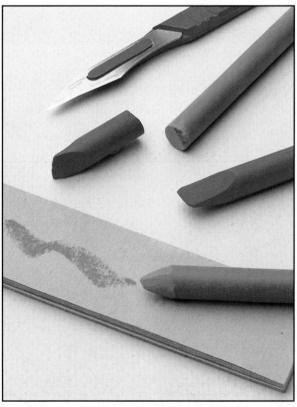
Round pastels - flat and pointed end

14

Demonstration 3

Using Black and White Pastels on Grey Paper

The dramatic and wonderful effects pastel can create are achieved with the minimum of materials. Here we look at the use of white and black pastel on grey paper. We use the white to identify the highlights and the black to identify the darkest shadows. The grey paper acts as the medium, or third tone.

Right. Take a piece of white pastel and draw the wineglass shown here.

Below. Now draw the glass again putting in the white highlights, then add the black pastel. Likewise try the saucepan, the shiny metal bowl and spoon, then the candle and candlestick holder. Don't let the black and white pastel mix on the paper when trying this demonstration or the resulting colour will be grey.

Look around your home for similar articles such as teapots or coffee pots, cups and saucers, mugs or ornaments you could try to sketch using this technique.

HANDY HINT. Have a strong source of light shining on the objects from the left or right. This will help emphasise the highlights and the strong shadows.

A white on grey study

Black and white pastel studies

Demonstration 4
Still life: Black and White Pastel

Staying with the black and white pastels on grey paper, let us progress from single objects to a still life composition. The group consists of a wine bottle, wineglass and bowl of fruit set against a pink drape and standing on a checked tablecloth.

Stage 1. I have used square pastels on this occasion, but round pastels are equally suitable. I normally suggest a subject is sketched in light outline with white pastel, or a 2B pencil. This ensures the subject is correctly drawn and provides a sound foundation for your picture. Many pastel artists like drawing in the way seen here. Use the side and top edge of your pastel to shape the objects. Using the side of your black pastel, lightly add the tone of each item you see, including the background drape and the tablecloth.

Stage 2. The light is coming from the right side. The darker tones and shadows will be on the left of the objects. Using a little extra pressure on your pastel, add the medium tones to those areas.

Stage 3. Still using the side of the pastel, add the darker tones to the drape and wine bottle. NOW USE THE SIDE AND TIP OF THE WHITE PASTEL to add the highlights. Finally use the top-edge of your black pastel to draw in the line and details of the fruit. Use stippling (dots) to create the effect of the orange skin. Add the line and details to the glass bowl, wine bottle, wineglass and tablecloth.

Stage 1

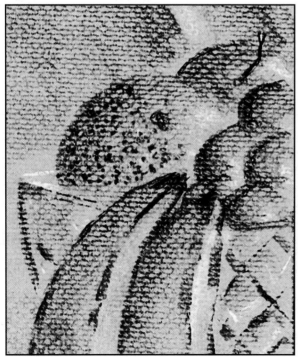
Detail

Stage 2

16

Stage 3.

Demonstration 5
Landscape
Black and White

Stage 1

For our last black and white demonstration let us think about the outdoors and progress to a simple landscape. The subject consists of a pathway leading to a cottage, with trees to the right and distant trees, a lake and hills beyond the cottage.

Stage 1. Sketch the subject with a 2B pencil. Using the side of a piece of white pastel, sketch in the white of the sky, sunlit lake, highlights on the trees, cottage, fields, fence and path.

Stage2. Using a piece of black pastel, add the pale and medium tones to the hills, trees, roof, path, fields and fence.

Stage 2

Stage 3. With the top edge of your black pastel, or top corner of a square black pastel, pick out the detail of the stonework on the cottage, right-hand trees, path and fence.

After these first demonstrations you will be surprised how much control and dexterity you are beginning to achieve just using two pastels. This work provides an excellent foundation for your future pastel sketching and painting.

HANDY HINT. With landscape subjects, paths, roadways, hedges, rustic walls and fences can be useful to help lead people's eyes into the picture.

Stage 3

Demonstration 6
Venetian Bridge: Monochrome

Stages 1, 2, 3 and 4. With the pastel sketching technique, the colour of the paper used can play an important role in the overall look of the picture. Here I use a cream pastel paper with a sanguine, reddish-brown, square pastel. A round pastel of a similar colour could also be used. Hold a medium - sized piece of the pastel with its side flat to the paper, and, in the centre of the page, make a sweeping upward curve for the under-side of the bridge. Add the softer tones to the left and the right of the bridge opening and the darker stone slabs of the top of the bridge. With downward strokes add the first tones of the buildings and with angled strokes add the canal walls.

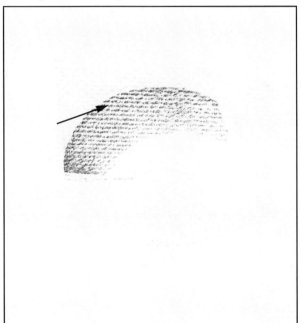

Stage 1

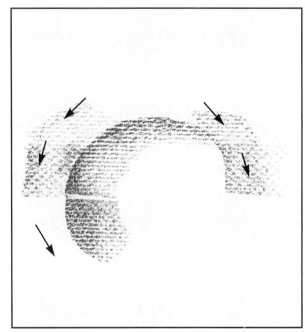

Stage 2

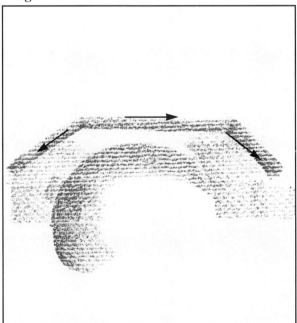

Stage 3.

Stage 4

Stage 5. Continuing with the side of the pastel, but with a little extra pressure and with shorter strokes, add the start of the windows and shutters. Using the top edge of the pastel, pick out the more distant windows, the edges of the roof tiles and the lines denoting the stone slabs on top of the canal walls. Take great care not to let the side of your hand, wrist, shirt or blouse sleeve catch and smudge the surface of your pastel picture.

With the top edge of the pastel, add the lines and detail to the windows and shutters, church, bridge railings and canal walls. Finally a few sweeping lines on the canal will give the reflections of the canal walls and the bridge.

Stage 5

Finished study

Demonstration 7
The Doorway: Pastel Study

Now is an ideal time to begin using some of the many wonderful coloured pastels you will find in pastel sets. Doors and entrances often make excellent subjects.

Stage 1. Use a piece of white pastel to block in the main shape of the door, doorstep, pavement and potted plant.

Stage 2. With the side of a piece of yellow pastel block in the front door. With the side of a piece of white pastel hint at the white painted wall. Using a grey pastel and a ruler add the grey lines on the door and a hint of grey in the glass window above the door. With green and brown block in the potted plants. Use a grey pastel on its side to block in the path.

Stage 3. Use the top edge of a black pastel just to outline the top overhang of the door, the detail in the windows and the overhang supports to the left and right of the door. Use a ruler and a dark brown pastel to carefully add the lines for the four doorpanels. Pick out the outline of the step in grey. Use a little black to suggest the edges of the paving stones. Pick out the darker green and darker browns of the plants and pots. Add the door knocker, letter box and door handle. The coloured pastel study is now finished.

Stage 1

Stage 2

Stage 3

Demonstration 8
Sunflower

Pastels allow artists to produce very delicate or very bold work and give freedom for individual styles. In this demonstration I deliberately selected black pastel paper as I knew that the yellow, brown and green of a sunflower would look very striking against it.

Stage 1. Draw the sunflower outline in yellow pastel. The leaves and stem should be drawn in green.

Stage 2. Fill in the petals with yellow. On this occasion the black outlines add to the very dramatic style of the picture. Put a little green on the central circle, then stipple reddish brown and black pastel to develop the striking centre of the flower. Use a light and medium green for the leaves and stem.

Stage 3. The leaves and stem can have the line and detail added with yellow and black pastel. The sunflower can simply be left with the contrasting black background or a background of your choosing can be added. I have put in the blue sky. Be adventurous, experiment and play with ideas and images.

Coloured pastels used

Stage 1

Stage 2

Stage 3

Demonstration 9

Pointillism

Georges Seurat, the French artist, developed a technique of painting pictures using dots of paint, dots of colour. This technique became known as Pointillism. In this demonstration I have used the candle and candlestick holder from one of the earlier demonstrations to practice this technique.

Stage 1. Sketch the subject out lightly using white pastel.

Stage 2. Stipple the white candle, white with dots of grey in the areas away from the flame. Using first yellow, then orange, then red and then mauve pastel, stipple the candlestick holder and candle flame in the way shown in the detail panel. Use white, then yellow for the highlights, then pale and dark blue for the colour of the background drape and its shadows.

Stage 3. Use yellow, light green and dark green for the tablecloth. Use dark green and black dots under the base of the candlestick holder. I have shown the three stage build-up of the main features of this picture in the detail panel.

Stage 1

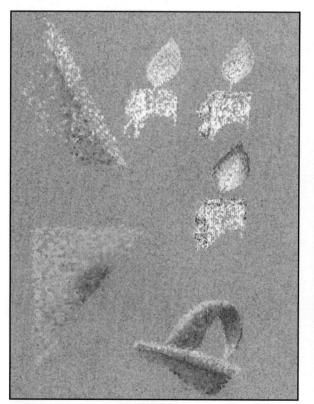

Detail

Stage 2

24

Stage 3

Demonstration 10
Still Life - Colour

Having tried out the previous demonstrations in this book you will now be beginning to understand the nature and possibilities of pastels.

In an earlier part of the book I referred to the difference between PASTEL SKETCHING and PASTEL PAINTING. Here is an opportunity to use an exciting range of colours and to try the PASTEL SKETCHING technique on a still life subject. Remember that with pastel sketching the pastel is not rubbed and blended with the finger. It is applied directly to the paper surface and the background colour is allowed to show through to become an integral part of the finished pastel sketch.

The subject is a bowl of fruit, a wine bottle and a wineglass on a blue checked tablecloth with a pinkish mauve drape in the background. The lines of the folds of the hanging drape and the perspective lines of the tablecloth lead our eyes from all four corners of the picture to our main subject on the table.

The bottle gives height to the composition, the bowl of fruit slightly to one side and behind the bottle and the overhanging bananas help to add depth. There is a lively colour interest. The light source is coming from the right-hand side.

Stage 1. Use a warm grey pastel paper and sketch the subject out with a piece of white pastel. Try to ensure that the bottle and wineglass are vertical and do not lean to one side or the other. This can be checked by turning the sketch upside down. Any leaning lines can be checked and corrected as simply as that.

Stage 2. To ensure that you do not smudge what you are sketching, work from top to bottom, left to right if you are right-handed. If you are left-handed, work from top to bottom, right to left. Snap a piece of pale pink pastel, side on, to lay in the shadow areas of the folds in the drape. The highlights on the drape can be picked out with pale pink.

Stage 1

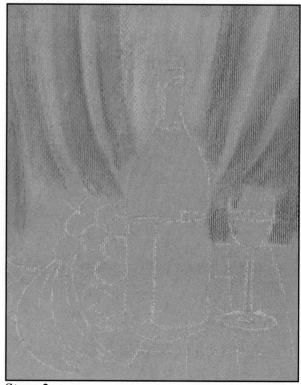

Stage 2

Still Life Detail

Stage 3

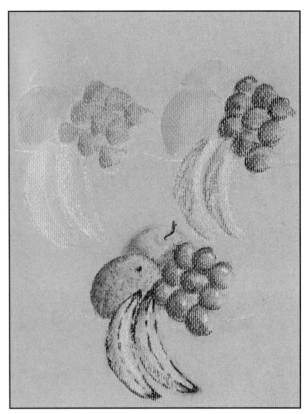

Stage 4

Stage 3. Using medium green, yellow, white and black build up the wine bottle in the three stages shown. Apply the medium green, then pick out the yellowish green. For the very dark green area, use green superimposed with black. Use white to pick out the highlights. Using white and medium grey pick out the label shapes. The label details can be added with red, green and black.

Stage 4. The fruit in the glass bowl and the wineglass can be built up in a similar manner. With the fruit, watch especially for the stippling, that is, dotting of the pastel on the orange skin, the dark black ends to the banana, the rich dark shadow and the highlights on the grapes.

Stage 5. When building up the wineglass, the darker red of the wine is made by superimposing black on red. Also emphasise the darkest parts of the wineglass and the sharp white highlights. Finally, add the checked tablecloth, using pale blue for the cloth with a darker blue to draw in the lines of the pattern.

Stage 5

Finished still life

Demonstration 11
Landscape

Landscape subjects provide good material for the pastel artist. The versatility of pastels enables one to capture the changing seasons of spring, summer, autumn and winter. We are surrounded by a wealth of differing landscapes, both in our own country and abroad. Pastels can enable one to capture all manner of landscape moods, from gentle atmospheric landscape to the bright colourfulness of a sunset, from a snow-covered landscape to green fields and trees on a warm summer's afternoon.

Using the pastel sketching technique, I show here and over the page how to create a landscape sketch in colour on a bluish-grey pastel paper.

Stage 1. You can either choose to lightly sketch out the subject in white pastel, or to work freehand, putting the sky in first and then building up the landscape.

Stage 2. Using the sides of white, then light blue and dark blue pastels, create the sky, leaving parts of the paper showing through.

Stage 3. With the tips of light and medium green pastels and a reddish-brown for the copper beech tree, block in the first stages of light and dark for the trees and bushes. Using medium green, light blue and white pastels with sideways sweeping pastel strokes, start the river, remembering again to leave parts of the paper showing.

Stage 4. With a darker green, pick out the darker tones of the green tree foliage and bushes. Use a darker brown for the copper beech tree foliage and tree trunks. With a dark green and reddish-brown, hint at the reflections of the tall, slim poplar trees and beech tree.

Stage 5. Using the top edge of your pastels complete the trcc reflections in the river and add the white highlights on the water. Use a stick of green pastel to draw in the grasses in the foreground corners of the picture. With light brown, dark brown and white draw in the fence entering the river from the left-hand bank.

Stage 1

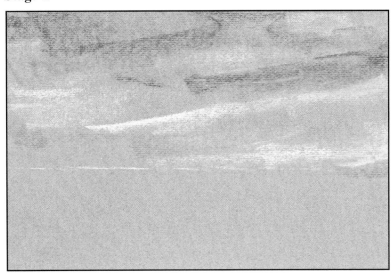
Stage 2

Stage 3

Stage 4

Stage 5
30

Demonstration 12
Seascape

Anyone who has stood close to the seashore and witnessed the sounds and colour of crashing, swirling sea will almost certainly have been moved or inspired by it. The sea can be a dramatic subject, one which I often encourage people who attend my art courses to try.

Stage 1. Sketch out the subject with white pastel.

Stage 2. Use white and light blue for the main sky. Superimpose a little dark blue on the darker clouds to the left and right. Ensure the horizon is quite light. Use pale blue and white for the distant sea and waves beyond the rock. Start the rocks with a cream and a medium brown pastel.

Stage 3. Add a darker brown and then a little black pastel to the rocks. Use light and dark blue, a little black and then white to create the swirling, wavy foreground sea.

Details of stages 2, 3 and 4 can be seen in the detail panel over the page.

Stage 4. The line and detail of the rocks are picked out with the side and tip of a black pastel. The effect of the white sea foam splashing upwards behind the right - hand rocks is created by stippling with a white pastel. The white crests of the foreground waves are also added with a white pastel.

HANDY HINT. Try to imagine what it would look, sound and feel like standing by this seascape. The sea is constantly moving. You can hear the sounds of the sea crashing against the rock and you can feel the wind. Try to capture that feeling in your picture.

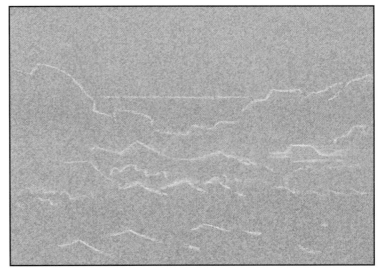

Stage 1

Stage 2

Stage 3

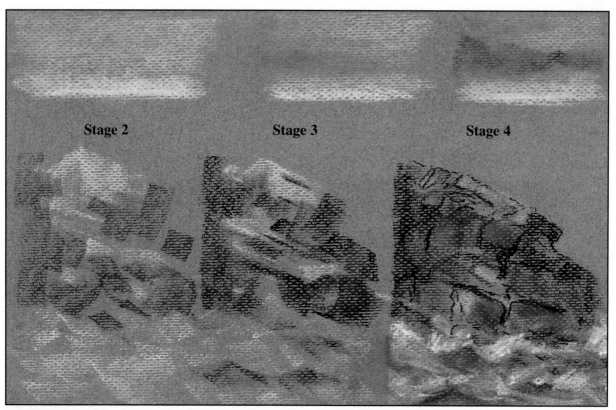

Detail panel

Stage 4

Demonstration 13
Pastel Painting

The demonstrations so far have concentrated on PASTEL SKETCHING. The art of PASTEL PAINTING which we now explore enables you to use your fingers to smudge and blend the pastels, one on top of the other. Pastel sketching uses the colour of the paper as a feature of the sketch. In pastel painting the pastel obliterates the colour of the paper. The blue ball clearly demonstrates the pastel painting technique.

Stage 1. Draw the ball outline in white pastel. Pick up your pastels and place light blue, medium blue and dark blue as in the areas shown in the demonstration.

Stage 2. Gently rub and blend the patches of pastel colour together using the tip of a clean finger.

Stage 3. Add the yellow and orange background, blending them with your finger. Add the shadow on the table with a little dark brown and black.
Your fingers will become quite messy with colour from the pastels, so remember to have a clean, damp flannel in a polythene bag by your side; this will enable you to keep wiping your fingers clean. Mistakes can be removed, and corrections made, by gently jabbing at the surface of the paper with a clean, dry brush to dislodge the loose pastel which you blow off the picture surface. A clean putty eraser can be used to rub away the remaining area of colour, thus avoiding the pastel smearing.

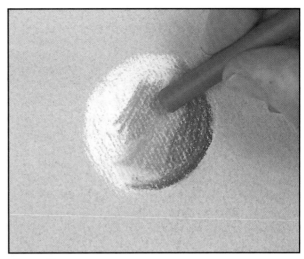
Stage 1

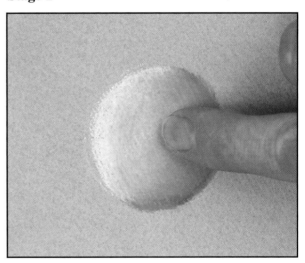
Stage 2

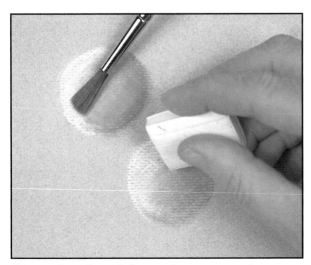
How to brush and then rub away pastel.

Stage 3

33

Demonstration 14
Landscape

This landscape provides a very good subject to help you quickly understand the technique of blending pastels.

Stage 1. Sketch out the landscape using white pastel on a medium grey paper.

Stage 2. Using pieces of pastel on their sides, pastel in bold strokes of white, medium blue and dark blue for the sky. They may be strokes of different length. Lay on the paper sweeping side strokes of grey, blue and mauve for the hills. Apply light sweeping side strokes of medium yellow, light green and medium green pastel for the fields. Using light pressure, superimpose a few white strokes on the green fields, just to give a hint of white. Add darker green patches of pastel on the tree and bush areas. Be generous with the pastel, put lots on the paper.

Stage 3. Go in turn to the sky, hills and fields and gently rub and blend the areas of colour with a fingertip. Rub and blend the bushes and trees after the blending of the field areas. Gradually the colour will obliterate the background colour of the paper. A smoother look, quite different to that seen in the pastel sketching technique, should now be observed.

Detail. In the detail panel you will see the build-up of stages 1 and 2. In that panel I also show how to use a darker green and the top edge of a round or square black pastel or a black pastel pencil to emphasise the line, form and bushiness of the trees and foliage.

Stage 4. In the finished pastel study, notice how the form and details have been added to all the trees and bushes. A white fence has also been added to the right corner area of the landscape to complete the picture.

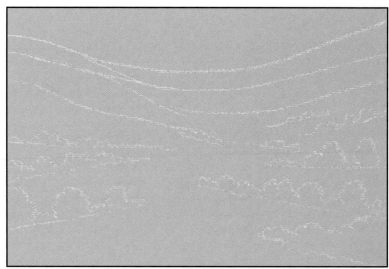

Stage 1

Stage 2

Stage 3

| Stage 1 | Stage 2 | Detail to trees and foliage |

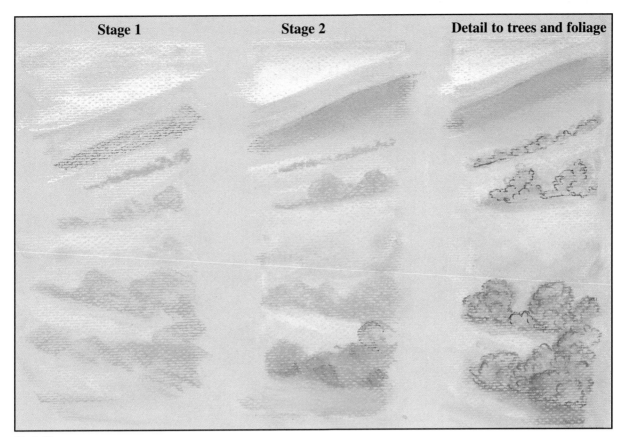

Detail

Stage 4

Demonstration 15
A Sunset

The fiery evening sunset takes us into a brighter, more vivid range of pastel colours. The subject provides some larger areas on which to practise pastel blending, yet offers the use of a silhouette for detail, and contrast between light and dark.

Stage 1. On this occasion, rather than sketch out the subject, create the sunset and reflection in the water first. Use white pastel for the sun, yellow and orange in the remaining areas, with just a little crimson red in all four corners of the page.

Stage 2. Blend the colours with your fingertip working from light to dark: white to yellow to orange to red.

Stage 3. Use the top edge of a black pastel or black pastel pencil, to lightly draw on the real and reflected body of the windmill, house, tree and bushes.

Detail. A. In the shapes created by the outline use diagonal strokes of brown pastel to fill in the silhouette in the sky and its reflection in the river. B. Press more heavily on the brown pastel. C. Use gentle black diagonal lines over the brown, blending with the tip of a finger or, if you wish, leaving it unblended in these areas. The choice is yours.

Stage 4. With a pointed black pastel or black pastel pencil, and a ruler, draw in the windmill sails. A little yellow can be used for highlights and also for the windows on the house. Using dark brown pastel and a black pointed pastel, pick out the boughs and branches of the tree. Use orange for the highlights on the tree. Complete the reflections with horizontal strokes of the pastel to add to the watery effect.

Stage 1

Stage 2

Stage 3

Detail A

Detail B   **Detail C**

Stage 4

Demonstration 16
Snow Scene

Those of us who live in areas where in the winter months snow falls, enjoy one of nature's great events. We see our familiar landscapes blanketed in white, offering us exciting and new subject possibilities. When the snow has fallen, there is a unique silence which gives the landscape its own special atmosphere. The mauvish - blue grey shadows play upon the white snowscape. Such views offer the artist very special opportunities.

Stage 1. Sketch out the subject with white pastel on a dark grey paper.

Stage 2A. (left - hand side) Lay on broad sweeping strokes of white and blue pastel for the sky. Use blue, white and grey pastel for the snow - covered mountains and fields. Use white and grey pastel with a patch of vivid green for the fir trees on the left - hand side.

Stage 2B. Rub and blend gently the pastel with your finger tip to create the blended effect seen here.

Stage 3. For the central areas use a sharpened black pastel, or a black pastel pencil, and the top edge of a brown pastel to pick out the detail of the trees, stone wall, barn and the grasses which peek through the foreground snow.

HANDY HINT. Because of the speed you can work with pastels they are excellent for outdoor sketching in cold weather. The sketches can provide useful material for indoor painting in any medium.

Stage 1 Outline

Stage 2 A   **Stage 2B**

Stage 3

Demonstration 17
Albert Tower

One of my favourite landscapes features the Albert Tower on the Isle of Man. The island sits in the Irish Sea midway between Great Britain and Ireland. The Albert Tower, in the north of the island, was built on high ground overlooking Ramsey Bay, on the spot where Queen Victoria and Prince Albert stood to admire the view on an official visit to the Isle of Man. This unique piece of Victorian architecture now houses high technology broadcasting aerials and equipment, proving that conservation and technology can go hand in hand.

Stage 1. Sketch out the subject in white pastel.

Stage 2. Block in the main areas of pastel colours for the sky using white, a little light blue and grey. Block in the mountains, hillside and foreground fields, using pale yellowish-greens superimposed with darker greens. Use and emphasise the brownish-black mix on the shaded left-hand side of the mountains. Block in the light and medium dabs of grey to suggest the stonework for the tower. Add the reddish-browns and beige for the featured stonework on the main tower and for the wood of the door.

Stage 3. Add the stronger medium and darker green tones to the trees and to the foreground grass. Use a black pastel pencil to pick out the detail to the stonework of the tower, wall and trees and foreground grass.

Stage 1. Outline

HANDY HINT.
If sketching or painting out of doors spend 10 to 15 minutes walking around your chosen view or subject as you may find an even better viewpoint. Don't just take the first viewpoint that catches your eye, even though you may choose that in the end.

Detail

Stage 2

Stage 3

41

Demonstration 18
Bridge over River

"Curved is the line of beauty, straight is the line of duty" is a favourite saying of mine when talking to art students. Much in nature is based on curved lines, circles and ovals, but so much of what man builds is based on straight lines. This subject combines straight and curved lines.

Stage 1. Sketch the outline of the subject in white.

Stage 2. By now you should be familiar with how to mass in the main blocks of colour for each area. So often people are skimpy with the amount of pastel they put on the paper. Don't be. With the pastel painting technique you really have to be prepared to use a substantial amount of pastel, especially the lighter colours.

Stage 3. Rub and blend the main areas of pastel so that all the paper is fully covered.

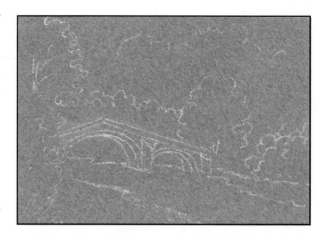

Stage 4. This is where you start to look for and develop the essential features and details: add stronger blue to sky and water, add the shadows under the bridge arches, the dark greens and highlights on the foliage, the highlights on the water, the foreground stones and rocks in the river.

Stage 2

42

Stage 3

Stage 4

Demonstration 19
Fruit and Vegetables

The French painter Cézanne once said that all the problems in painting were to be found in a bowl of apples. He drew and painted lots of them. Fruit and vegetables can provide a wealth of material, both for pastel sketching and pastel painting with great diversity of colour and surface texture. Many everyday objects we take for granted can often make great subjects. When next visiting a greengrocer or department store, look and think for a moment how you could create pictures from the items you see. It might be a study of a single apple, a selection spread on a table or a more complex grouping.

HANDY HINT. When painting fruit, vegetables or flowers which you are going to continue painting the next day, carefully wrap the subjects in polythene bags and place them in a refrigerator. They will retain their freshness longer.

Apple

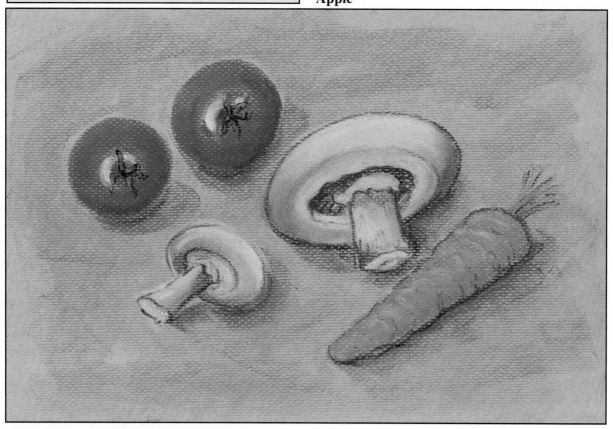

Mushrooms, tomatoes and carrots

44

Demonstration 20
Narcissus

In an earlier demonstration I showed a bold, free - flowing style of pastel sketching for the sunflower. In the demonstration of the Narcissus on this page I have used a gentler, pastel painting technique to give a more photographic look.

Stage 1. I plan to let the background paper provide the background colour for the flower to be seen against. Draw the outline shape in white on black paper.

Stage 2. Apply white and pale cream pastel for the petals, yellow and orange pastel for the centre, medium and light green for the leaf.

Stage 3. Blend the larger areas with a fingertip and the smaller areas with a tortillon or a stub. Apply a dark brown pastel very lightly, then blend the shadows. Use a black pastel pencil for the darker shades and key lines. Use a black pastel gently on the green, then blend it for the darker green shadows on the stem and back of the leaf.

Be prepared for an intriguing surprise when painting potted plants or cut flowers. They will change and alter before your eyes as you paint them. Flowers are living organisms. The time of day, changing light and warmth of the environment affects them, just as those conditions affect us.

HANDY HINT. Set light flowers against a dark background and dark flowers against a light background. If working indoors from life, ensure your subject has a good strong light coming from the left or right - hand side, either from a window or from an angled tablelamp.

Demonstration 21

Liquorice Allsorts

If ever there was a subject made for pastels, especially the square pastel, it must be liquorice allsorts. Open a box, scatter a few on a sheet of paper on the table in front of you and you have a subject in seconds. The square allsorts can be drawn in minutes using the wide side and narrow, top edge of a square pastel. The blue and pink allsorts towards the front of my picture, known as hundreds and thousands, can be captured with stippling. The larger, round allsorts can be created in the pastel painting technique. For the table I used light and medium blue pastels, with black for the shadows and for the liquorice. When finished you can enjoy the picture and eat the allsorts.

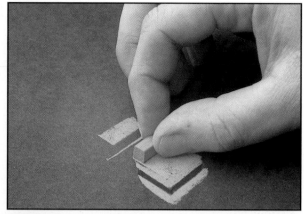

Detail

Liquorice Allsorts

Demonstration 22
Tinting Water Colour Paper for Pastels

Whilst pastel paper is normally coloured, it is also available in white. Exciting possibilities are open to you when using white 'NOT', slightly textured, or 'ROUGH' water colour paper, tinting it any colour or combination of colours, using water colours or acrylic paint. Suitable white water colour paper, Cotman or Winsor and Newton artist quality paper can be bought by the sheet or in sketch pad form.

Cut a sheet of the paper to the size you want. Using a strong gummed tape, stick all four sides of the paper to a wooden drawing board. Use a large flat water colour brush to apply a wash of water colour or acrylic paint of your choice to the paper. Let it dry naturally, or accelerate the drying by using a domestic hand - held hair dryer to blow warm air on the paper to evaporate the water. Any wavering of the paper should go as it normally dries flat.

'NOT' water colour paper

'ROUGH' water colour paper

Plain white water colour paper

Tinting water colour paper for pastels

Composition

The sketch or drawing of the subject you are going to paint, the skills in your colouring of it, the illusion of the textural effects, use of light and shade are all elements of your painting. Another equally important aspect to which I come now is the composition of a painting.

There are certain guidelines which, if followed, can help you build your work on sound compositional foundations. One of the most important things to avoid is having any line or object that cuts your picture into two equal halves, as in view A below, where the horizon is halfway and so divides the picture into equal horizontal halves, and in view B, where the tree trunk divides the view into two vertical halves. Set any such line or object to one side or other as in C and D. The horizon is just below halfway and the tree trunk to the left of halfway.

FOCAL POINTS AND KEY LINES

Decide what it is that you want the person looking at your painting to notice in particular. The eyes should not be left to wander as if the viewer is lost. You are the artist, you are in control, be decisive. A picture should have a FOCAL POINT, that is, a main feature to which the eyes are led. I show three views. In E, the Focal Point, the yacht, is in the middle distance, in F, the Focal Point, the bridge and group of houses, is in the far distance, and in G, the figure which is in the foreground is the focal point.

A picture should also have KEY LINES of the composition leading the eyes of the viewer to the FOCAL POINT. I have arrowed the key lines of the three compositions and I think from these illustrations you will see how the use of the Focal Point and Key Lines help bring a composition together.

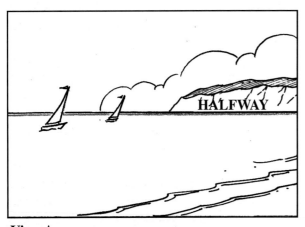

View A

View B

View C

View D

View E

View F

THE TRIANGLE

Very often the triangular composition can offer an excellent shape on which to base a composition, especially a still life or floral study. In the three illustrations H, I, and J, I show this at work.

In H, I have a still life made up from a vase of flowers and a book on a table by the window. I have placed the vase to the left, forming the left-side of the triangle; the open book forms the base of the triangle. In I, the shape of the dish holding the fruit adds to the triangular format of this subject, with the apex of the triangle just off-centre to the right. The seated figure to the right, in J, forms the upright side of the triangle. The figure's legs under the table help form the base of the triangle.

Try to ensure that still life and floral studies have height, width and depth.

If you now go and look at paintings or prints of paintings by any of the great masters, or by any fine artist of today, you will almost certainly find that their most successful paintings employ many of the important compositional points I have referred to here.

View G

View H

View I

View J

49

Perspective

Perspective is the one area of drawing and painting in which most people experience some degree of difficulty. When most people hear perspective mentioned they go to a bookshop or a library, obtain a book on the subject, flip through it, see lines shooting about all over the place and usually end up more confused than before they opened it. The secret is to keep the whole business of perspective as simple as possible, to remember a few basic rules, and to bear in mind that perspective is not something one masters all in one, two or three lessons. Learning about perspective is an on-going learning process. One goes along over a period of months, indeed years, collecting together the pieces of information, like pieces of a jigsaw, until they fit together and the picture, the theory of

colour, colour harmony and colour balance. I am pleased to say with the introduction of teaching technology to girls as well as boys at school this should change in the future.

The eyelevel is an imaginary line, horizontally across your field of vision when you look straight ahead, not up, nor down, but straight ahead. In my sketch I show a figure sitting low down, as if on a beach, then standing, then standing on a sand dune. Note how the eyelevel is always directly ahead of the figure. When looking at a real subject look straight ahead, hold a ruler straight out with the thin edge in front of, and across your eyes, and that is where your eyelevel is. Which comes first, the drawing in of the eyelevel or the object? Generally

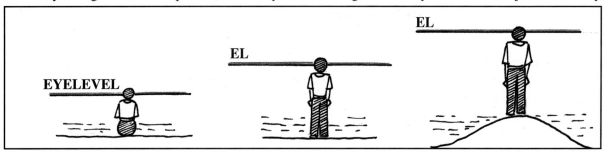

perspective, becomes clear and easy to apply to one's work. Most men used to have an advantage over the ladies when taking up drawing and painting, because at school most boys learned basic carpentry and even some metalwork. Some boys were taught basic technical drawing, and on leaving school and entering a working life the types of books, manuals and journals they read had line

I suggest you draw in the object lightly first, then apply the eyelevel and use it with the rules of perspective to check and correct the object.

One way to see perspective in action is to picture the view looking along railway lines. They appear to merge in the distance. The sleepers appear to become smaller and closer together. The point where the railway lines appear to merge is known

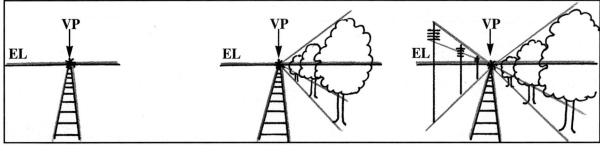

drawings, plans, front elevations and side elevations of all sorts of subjects in them. It is this basic familiarity with line that proved very useful when learning to paint. Most ladies don't have that background experience, so I often find ladies at first need more help with drawings. However, because of their knowledge from an early age of fashion, make-up and colour schemes I find ladies are far more advanced than men in relation to

as the "Vanishing Point", V.P. We know they do not merge in reality. I show this in my sketch. I also show the railway lines with telegraph poles on the left, then with three trees on the right. The telegraph poles and the trees in a drawing or painting would also appear to become smaller and closer together as they recede. I have shown the guidelines for each item, illustrating how the guidelines all meet at the Vanishing Points, V.P.

Next, I show a front view of a picnic basket. With this view we have just one vanishing point for the top sides of the basket placed on a table. I am imagining that you or I would be sitting on a normal dining room chair when drawing this basket, in which case, I think you would find your eyelevel would be just about 18"(450mm) above the back of the basket. In my next sketch the basket is set at an angle. Now we have two vanishing points, one for each side of the basket. Often guidelines want to converge on the eyelevel, but off the page. This is normal, and often happens. When it does, lay scrap paper at the side, tape it on from behind and extend

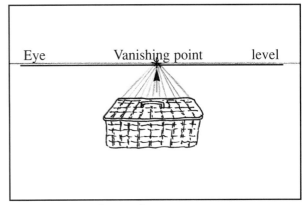

Picnic basket, front view

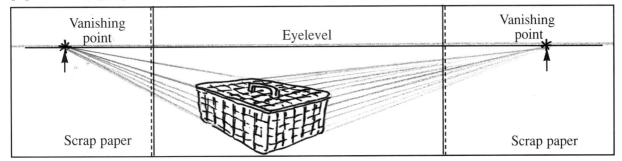

Picnic basket at an angle

the guidelines onto it, in the way I show in my sketch. Never guess or assume the perspective is correct, always try to 'prove' it.

Circular Perspective.

Few people realise that perspective can be used to help solve the problems of drawing circles and ellipses, but it can. I have illustrated this with a sketch of a bowl, a spaghetti jar and a rolling pin on its side. I have lightly drawn out the group and have placed my eyelevel well above it. I have then drawn a light guiding square around each ellipse we can see and have drawn those squares 'in perspective', in the same way as the basket has been drawn. The squares for the ellipses each have their respective vanishing points on the common eyelevel. The bowl and jar share the same vanishing point as their ellipses are on the same plane. The ellipse for the rolling pin is on a different plane so has its own vanishing point at a different position on the eyelevel. The use of the squares helps determine where each vanishing point should be, to ensure the true perspective of the subject where there is an ellipse involved. I then go back to each ellipse and check it touches the centre of each side of the square it occupies, for provided it does, I know the ellipse must be in perspective. The squares used outside of each ellipse and perspective guidelines can be rubbed out gently before a picture is shaded in or painted.

Modern Offices at an angle with 2 V.P.s

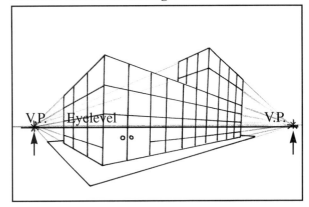

Circular perspective, kitchen utensils

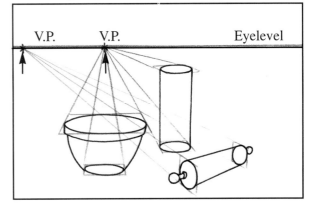

Demonstration 23
Pastel Pencils

Pastel pencils are a very popular way of creating pastel pictures. They are specially suitable for work in which detail is important. Pastel pencils can be used for a whole range of subjects. They can also be combined with the soft pastels used in the previous sections of this book. The pastel comes encased in wood. It has a pre-sharpened point. Apart from the facility to create detail easily, your fingers will generally remain clean due to the pastel's wooden casing.

Below right. As with all art materials it is important to spend a little time playing with the pastel pencils on some spare paper to see just what effects can be created. Pick up a pastel pencil and try creating the lines and effects you see in the bottom right-hand panel. Try hatching lines, crosshatching, stippling and traditional shading effects working from light to dark.

Opposite. I show a number of other ways to explore the potential of pastel pencils. Note and try the different hatching and crosshatching effects for the coloured balls. Draw the outline of the box, then draw it again and shade it in. Make experimental shading strips superimposing one colour on another. Note how subtle colour changes can be made as the colours overlap. Try creating the tile, brick and tree effects. Try creating the fish silhouettes and face just by using downward hatching lines. Experimenting in this way will be time well and wisely spent.

HANDY HINT. Do not try sharpening pastel pencils in a pencil sharpener as the tips will often snap off. Use a sharp knife to cut away the wood and then rub the exposed pastel on a sheet of glass paper to make the point into a round or chisel shape to suit your picture making needs.

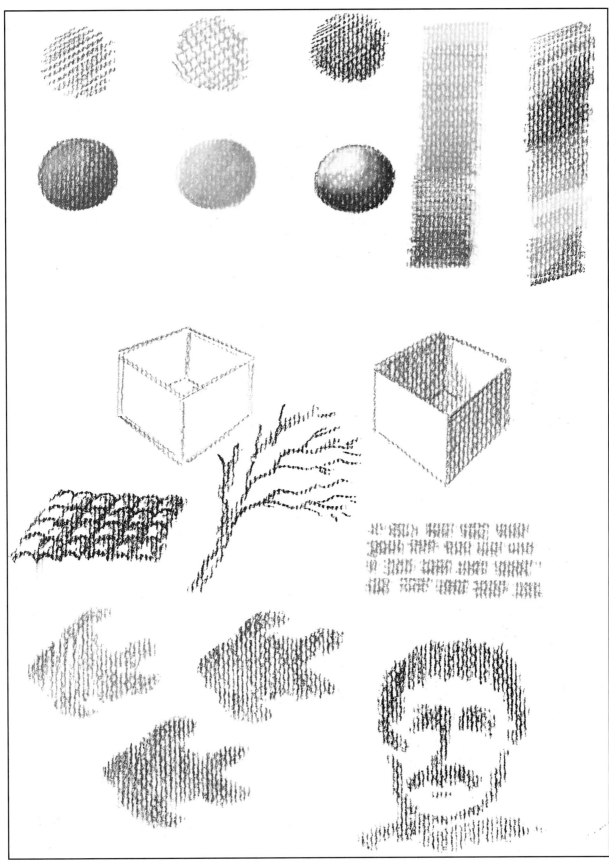

Pastel pencil effects for you to try

Demonstration 24
Bread and Cheese

A cut loaf, a piece of cheese and a bread knife are yet another example of how you can create interesting subjects by just looking around your home.

With pastel pencils I have used a hatching sketching technique to illustrate this subject.

Stage 1. On a sheet of light grey pastel paper sketch out the subject in white pastel pencil.

Stage 2. Using a light, creamy-beige for the outer bread crust build up diagonal hatching lines. The strength of tone of colour is controlled by the pressure you apply to the pastel. The heavier the pressure, the stronger the colour. The less the pressure, the softer the colour. Use the same method for the crust of the slice of bread. Use the light, creamy-beige pastel for the cheese. Show the white bread with white pastel. Hatch in the brown breadboard and knife still using diagonal hatching lines.

Stage 3. Using a Burnt Sienna, a reddish-brown pastel pencil, superimpose the warmer tones on the bread crust. Use a combination of gentle light brown and grey strokes to create the shadow side of the cheese. Superimpose darker brown lines on areas of the breadboard, with gentle black lines added on top of the shadows. Use a little grey on parts of the bread. Also use this technique for the slice of bread and the knife.

Stage 4. Pick out the darkest areas and emphasise these. Pay special attention to the texture of the bread crust and white bread areas and the detail on the knife. Do not forget to add the dark shadow under the front edge of the breadboard and the white flashes of highlight on the bread knife.

Stage 1

Stage 2

Stage 3

Stage 4

Still life

Demonstration 25
Bird

For this study I used the pastel painting technique. I applied much more of the pastel to each area of the picture, using the pastel pencil to blend the top colour into the bottom colour. A finger, a tortillon or a stub can also be used for blending. The essential detail was picked out at the end using resharpened pastel pencils.

Stage 1. Draw the bird in white pastel. Start to pastel in the main areas of colour.

Stage 2. Look at each area and use darker pastel tones to build up the deeper, darker areas. Use white on the lighter areas, still blending each area to create the lighter and darker tones for the head and body of the bird.

Stage 3. The pastel pencils now enable you to draw in the detail to the eye, beak, feathers and the pattern on the body. The detail on the webbed feet can be added with black pastel pencil.

Opposite page. Soft pastels combined with pastel pencils. For the study of the bottle and glass of Guinness I first created the brown bottle, glass and background using the pastel painting technique with my sticks of soft pastel, blended with my fingers in the manner described earlier in the book. The detail of the bottle labels was easy to add using my pastel pencils.

Stage 1

Stage 2

Stage 3

Demonstration 26
Portrait

The ability to use the sketching or pastel painting technique makes pastels an excellent medium for portraiture. The main blocks of colour for the face and hair can be created by blending the colours, whilst pastel pencils make the addition of details such as the eyes, nose, ears and mouth quite easy.

Stage 1. For the study of the young man sketch the outline in white pastel pencil. Then use generous amounts of red, yellow ochre and white pastel pencils on the face and neck. Likewise apply light and dark brown to the hair in the way shown.

Stage 2. Blend the pastel strokes of the face and neck with a finger. Shadows to the flesh can be added by superimposing a little strong deep green and gently blending that into the flesh colour to create deeper flesh tones. With a clean finger blend the colours of the hair.

Stage 3. Use the pastel pencils to pick out the detail of the eyes, detail and shadow of the nose, nostril and the lips. The top lip is always a darker tone of red, with the highlight on the lip because that usually catches the light. The lines and contours of the hair can now be added, applying the lighter lines first, then the darker lines.

Stage 4. Add the shirt collar and jacket collar using a blending technique. Use an incomplete sketched look for the rest of the jacket. This will keep the emphasis on the main part of the picture, the face.

Stage 1

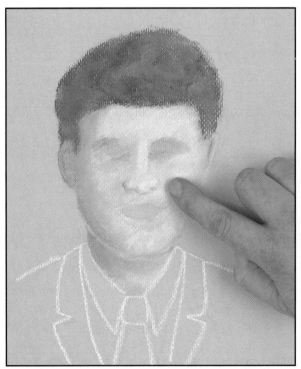

Stage 2

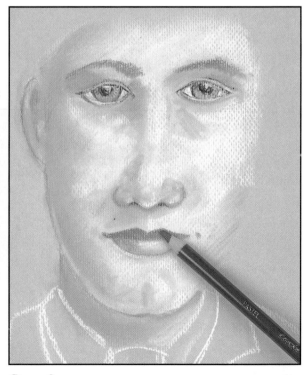

Stage 3

Stage 4

Demonstration 27

Oil Pastels

Oil pastels are very different to soft, chalk pastels and pastel pencils. They are oil based and will not mix with soft pastels. They are normally used on their own and have quite different properties to soft pastels.

Most art shops stock oil pastels, usually in sets, but sometimes loose as individual colours. Oil pastels normally have a paper wrapper to keep the fingers clean. However this can be peeled off to enable the side of the pastel to be used for placing larger areas of colour on the paper.

Oil pastels can be used in stick form to draw lines, or to shade in larger areas of colour. They can be superimposed on top of one another to create colour mixtures and blended effects. Red on yellow will create orange, blue on yellow will create green. They can also be blended with a soft sable or synthetic hair brush and turpentine. The artist dips the brush in a little clean turpentine and brushes over the area of oil pastel on the paper to dissolve the paint and blend it, or move it around, in a semi-fluid state to achieve different effects.

Whilst oil pastels can be used on canvas or canvas board, I find they work best on normal thick cartridge paper. If using turpentine to blend them, a colourless damp stain appears on the paper. This disappears as the turpentine evaporates from the paper.

Try the dry oil pastel lines and effects and then the blended effects shown in the right-hand panels.

Opposite page. Here I show the build-up of a banana. With the banana in panel A I used the dry pastel sketching technique. In panel B I used the brush-blended technique. In each example I start with yellow, then add a little green for the shadow and the black for the ends and marks on the skin. Trying these exercises will introduce you to the key techniques of oil pastels which you can try in other subjects.

HANDY HINT. If using a brush for blending, when finished wash the hairs with warm soapy water, cleaning them thoroughly then shake the brush dry. Stand it upright in a jar to enable the hairs to dry completely.

Oil pastels

Lines and effects

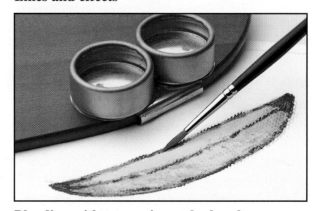

Blending with turpentine and a brush

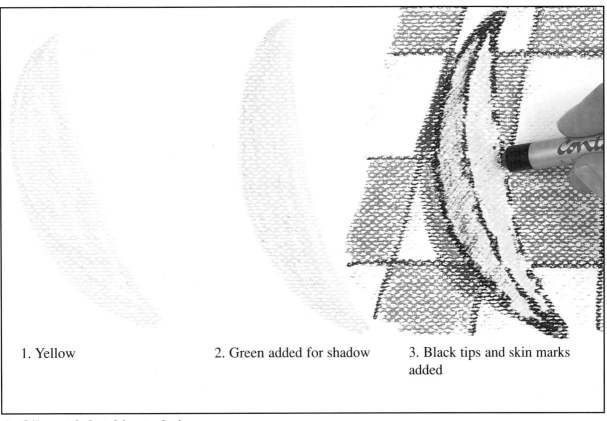

1. Yellow   2. Green added for shadow   3. Black tips and skin marks added

A. Oil pastel sketching technique

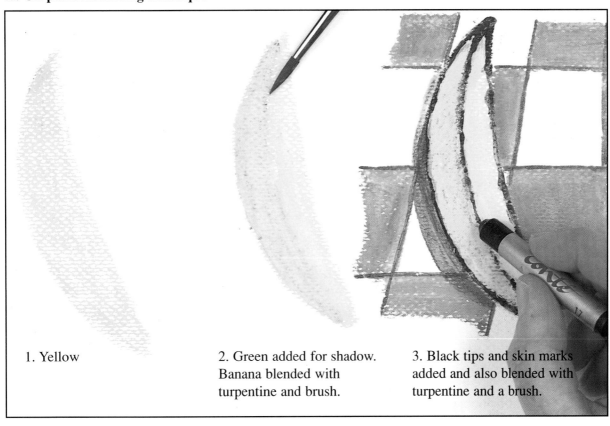

1. Yellow   2. Green added for shadow. Banana blended with turpentine and brush.   3. Black tips and skin marks added and also blended with turpentine and a brush.

B. Oil pastel brush-blended technique

Fixing and Framing Pastels

To prevent soft pastel and pastel pencil pictures from smudging there is wisdom in giving each picture a light spray of pastel fixative. Clear fixative is obtainable in ozone-friendly aerosol cans from art stores. Do not use this on oil pastels.

Lay newspaper on a table in a well-ventilated room. Hold the can of fixative 18" (45cm) above the picture and lightly spray it from left to right, top to bottom. Do not over spray the picture. Any slight dampness will go as the fixative evaporates. A sheet of acid-free, greaseproof paper can be laid over a dry pastel picture and held in place with paperclips in each corner. This prevents the transfer of colour to the backs of other pictures. The finished work can be stored flat in a portfolio.

Whilst some people like to make their own frames, most people take them to a professional picture framer. Pastels are best framed in the same manner as a water colour. Select a complementary colour of mount and a suitable frame moulding. A good framer will help and advise you if you ask him or her. The window mount provides a border round the picture and an air-space so the glass does not sit on the surface of the picture. A sheet of hardboard is used for the back and the assembled picture is ready for you to hang. Remember do not fix oil pastel pictures, but otherwise frame them as above.

Fixative for pastel pictures.

Backing board, picture, mount, glass and frame before final assembly.

Selling And Exhibiting Your Work

You will almost certainly want to keep for yourself, or give away as presents to family and friends, the first pictures you create. But if you have ever walked around an art gallery, or have seen paintings for sale, I would like to think you might, in time, be tempted to try exhibiting and selling some of your own work.

You may be aware of local art galleries where you live. The first thing to do is to find out which have "open" exhibitions. These are shows where any painter can send in one or more original paintings. Normally work will be chosen by a selection committee and you will be notified if yours is accepted or rejected. Some exhibitions will show all work submitted. It is an exhilarating feeling to go to an art gallery and to see work that you have produced hanging in an exhibition. It is also interesting to hear what other people say to one another when they come to a picture you have produced.

Work can often be exhibited and offered for sale in local retail stores such as furniture stores, post offices, shop windows, cafés and restaurants. This usually comes down to you talking to managers and proprietors of such establishments and

An artist viewing her exhibited picture

showing examples of your work. A percentage, from 10% to 33%, is normally requested by an establishment if a picture sells, in return for the display facility. Work can of course be offered for sale in most art exhibitions you enter. If a picture is "not for sale" mark it NFS.

Pricing work can prove tricky and the price will depend on the locality where the work is shown. A good local art gallery director, or picture framer, will often give you guidance, if you ask.

The opening of the annual Southport Palette Club Exhibition

PASTEL PAINTING

Philip Berrill
"The Flying Artist"
News Letter

is one of a series of art books which we hope you find helpful, enjoyable and informative.

The first four titles in the series are:
Everyone's Guide to...WATER COLOUR PAINTING
Everyone's Guide to...OIL PAINTING
Everyone's Guide to...PASTEL PAINTING
Everyone's Guide to...SKETCHING

These titles are available from bookshops and art shops or can be ordered direct from:

Sales Division
Philip Berrill International Ltd.
P.O. Box 39, Southport
PR8 4ZZ, England
e.mail: philipberrill@hotmail.com

If you would like to receive copies of Philip Berrill "The Flying Artist" Newsletters giving details of his demonstrations, talks, roadshows, painting holidays, videos and other interesting news please write to:

PHILIP BERRILL "THE FLYING ARTIST"
P.O. Box 39
Southport
PR8 4ZZ
England

Some helpful Do's and Don'ts

1. **Do play and experiment with your pastels to explore the wide range of marks and effects that can be achieved.**

2. **Do cover the table you are working on with old newspapers.**

3. **Do remember to use a dry paintbrush and a putty rubber to dust off and rub away any areas of pastel needing correction.**

4. **Do keep a damp flannel in a polythene bag by you to keep wiping your fingers clean.**

5. **Do try round, square and pencil pastels so that you learn the characteristics of each type.**

6. **Don't mix soft pastels and oil pastels. Use the oil pastels separately.**

7. **Don't use too much fixative to spray your pastel picture.**

8. **Don't forget that some of the best subjects are to be found in everyday objects and everyday situations.**

9. **Don't forget to use a window mount when framing your pastels under glass.**

10. **Don't let your pastels become damp; store them in a warm room.**

Remember ...if you have ever said "I wish I could paint" my message to you is
IF YOU WANT TO...YOU CAN